The Social Media Cookbook

Strategic Marketing Recipes for Small Business Success

Christina Kettman

Published by
Stairstep Press

ISBN: 978-0-9983320-0-0

LCCN: 2016918769

Cover and interior design by Tony Richardson, Adoration Design Services: adorationllc.com

Developmental editing by Debra Eckerling, Write On Online: writeononline.com

Copy editing by Shannon Luders-Manuel, shannonludersmanuel.com

CONTENTS

For my wonderful kids, Ben, Lily and Sam. Thanks for your patience as I scribbled out this book in the waiting room of dance classes, voice lessons, sports events, and all the time crevices of a multitasking-mom-life.

And for my husband Seann who inspires me daily.

Intro to the Social Media Cookbook

Many small business owners today struggle to figure out how to make social media work. Maybe they jumped onto Facebook or Twitter because someone told them they needed a company page, but now they never update it and have no idea what to do next. Every day they're hearing how social media is the next "must have" marketing strategy, and they're worried about missing out on big sales, and maybe even driving customers away with their lukewarm social media presence. Does any of that sound familiar? Then I have some good news: this book is for you!

I wrote this book specifically for small business owners who want to know how to do social media in a way that counts. It's called the Social Media Cookbook because cooking is something we all know and understand, and effective social media marketing—like good cooking—requires a solid knowledge base and a dash of creative inspiration.

Chapters 1-4 cover fundamental cooking techniques for each of the four major social media platforms: Facebook, LinkedIn, Twitter, and Instagram. Chapter 5 covers video platforms, including Periscope, Snapchat and YouTube. In Chapters 6-8, I introduce some organizing principles for putting together an effective social media campaign, including marketing to your ideal customer and developing calendars to stay organized. Finally, in Chapter 8, I provide some sample "recipes": case studies of successful social media campaigns at different budget levels and for different types of small businesses. The world of social media is moving at a rapid pace, but the principles I cover in these chapters do not.

My goal is simple: to give you enough know-how and creative ideas to consistently cook up a social media strategy that works for your small business. Now... Let's Get Cooking!

Get the Complimentary Social Media Marketing Checklist Free

Looking for a way to organize and follow through with all the action items from The Social Media Cookbook? Simply go to bit.ly/SMCookbookList and download the free Social Media Marketing Checklist to help you get started cooking with social media.

Stay on Top of the Many Social Media Marketing Changes

Time moves fast and so does social media. To help you keep up with this rapidly changing industry, I will post periodic updates to The Social Media Cookbook on my website. Bookmark the page at bit.ly/SMCookbookUpdates

Keep an eye out for these special highlights and tips:

Head Chef

All head chefs have their tricks of the trade. These sections give examples of what has worked for larger brands and businesses.

Who Knew?!

We have all been a "kitchen beginner" at one time or another. These sections share some surprising lessons I learned as I entered the world of social media marketing.

Key Ingredients

Sometimes you just need to keep essential ingredients on hand to make your meals a success. These boxes give you the key ingredients for image sizing, character limits and other social media components.

Kitchen Tools

In your real kitchen, you have helpful tools like blenders, toasters and chopping knives to make your cooking easier. In social media marketing, there are some helpful tools too. You'll find them in sections with this icon.

Chapter 1
Facebook: It's What's for Breakfast

2.23 billion monthly active users

f

68% of US adults are on Facebook

Check Please!

75% of US adults earning over $75,000 per year use Facebook

Sources: http://www.pewinternet.org/2018/03/01/social-media-use-in-2018/ ; https://www.statista.com/statistics/264810/number-of-monthly-active-facebook-users-worldwide/. Accessed October 8, 2018.

FACEBOOK MENU

Breakfast served 24 hours a day!

Intro to Facebook

PAGE + PROFILE

POSTING

MONITOR FACEBOOK
TO IMPROVE YOUR RECIPES

MY FAVORITE DISH:
FACEBOOK LIVE

Intro to Facebook

Facebook is the breakfast of social media for small businesses: it's the most important meal of the day. Don't skip it! This section gives you the information you need to set up an effective Facebook home page for your small business and create posts that resonate with your target audience. I'm sure you'll "like" it. (Sorry, I couldn't resist.)

The flavor of Facebook

People use Facebook to connect, be entertained, share and learn. So when businesses jump into the Facebook space and blare out a sales pitch, it's not surprising no one responds. By sharing interesting, entertaining and valuable content, you can get into conversations, foster relationships and connect with your customers.

Should Facebook be on your menu?

The audience on Facebook is so wide and varied that most businesses need some kind of presence, especially if they have a consumer market. Potential customers will check to see if your business has a Facebook page before searching for you on any other social platform. If you are looking for a place to get started with social media marketing, this is it.

Facts and figures

The world of Facebook is immense. As of June 2018, Facebook has 2.23 billion monthly active users, according to its website. As shown by the bar graph, people of all ages are on Facebook, with a high percentage of people age 18 to 49 being active.[1]

Nearly 70% of Americans use Facebook and three-quarters of them access Facebook on a daily basis.

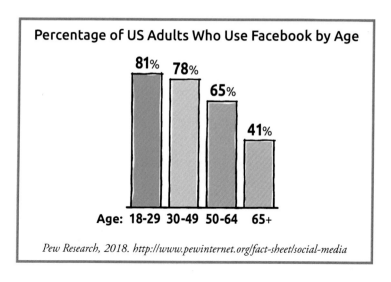

Percentage of US Adults Who Use Facebook by Age

81% · 78% · 65% · 41%

Age: 18-29 30-49 50-64 65+

Pew Research, 2018. http://www.pewinternet.org/fact-sheet/social-media

Your Facebook Business Page

Facebook is the go-to platform for most small businesses and is one of the easiest entry points to kick off your social media marketing. In fact, 67% of marketers choose Facebook as the most important platform, according to Social Media Examiner's "Social Media Marketing Industry Report."[2] This section will walk you through the components for creating your business page on Facebook and aligning it with your brand.

Determine your Facebook goals

You would never start cooking a meal without knowing what kind of dish you're trying to make and what kind of flavors to use—savory spicy or sweet (yum). The same is true with your business Facebook page: before you start throwing ingredients in a pot and set it to boil, you need to take a step back, figure out what you want to accomplish and pinpoint your specific goals. Anytime you embark on a marketing campaign, whether it be a direct mail postcard or social media page, you should have some goals in mind. Do you want to use Facebook to build your brand? Do you want to educate potential customers about your industry, product offering or niche? Do you want to drive traffic to your website? Write down all of the goals you want to accomplish through Facebook. Every post you share should contribute to at least one of those goals.

Common Facebook Goals for Small Businesses

Answer these questions to see if they match your goals:

- Are you trying to increase customer awareness of your business, products or services?
- Are you looking for ways to drive traffic to your website?
- Do you want Facebook to help you generate new leads?
- Are you looking to position yourself as a thought leader / expert in your industry?
- Do you need to extend your brand reach?
- Are you trying to learn more about your customers?

Make a good first impression

Customers may discover you on Facebook in a variety of ways: by clicking on an icon on your website, by seeing a "Like us on Facebook" sign in the offline world and then going online to check out your page, or simply by searching for your brand on Google and having it pop up. Chances are your Facebook page will be the first place customers get a taste of your social media brand. Just like in the real world, you need to make a good first impression. From the moment customers scan your page, they need to "get" your company's style. Are you serious and thoughtful? Educational? Humorous? Fun? What kinds of topics are you discussing on your page? Are you posting enticing videos and images to encourage customers to learn more? You want new page visitors to come away with a positive first impression of your brand.

Choose a template that fits your business

Facebook now offers you a variety of template choices for your page. When Facebook first rolled out Pages everyone got the Standard template, so you may not even be aware of the other choices. The current choices are Standard, Business, Services, Venues, Movies, Nonprofit, Politicians, Restaurants & Cafe, Shopping, and Video Page. Each one is designed to give your followers the best information about your business type, buttons on the toolbar, and a variety of tabs. The biggest difference between the templates is the layout and the tab choices. For example, the Restaurant & Cafe template has a primary button to get directions to the location and the layout is designed to highlight photos and important information about the menu, hours, and location.

To decide which template is best for your business go into your Page Settings and Page Edit, where you will find the place to edit your template.

Create a powerful profile and cover photo

Whether you call it an avatar or a profile photo, this 160 x 160 pixel image is the main face of your business. This image "follows" you throughout the Facebook world when you comment or share something. Most companies use a company logo, but you can use a headshot if you are building your personal brand. Do not make frequent changes to your profile photo. It should be familiar, memorable and representative of your business.

Your cover image acts as a backdrop for your page. Every Facebook user who follows your page will be alerted in their news stream when you change out your cover image. This is a simple way to remind your followers about your brand. Like your profile photo, your cover image should represent your company or brand. Design your image with a seasonal promotion or theme in mind and include your company name, tagline and URL.

Key Ingredients: Company Page Images

- Profile image: 180 x 180 pixels
- Cover image: size 820 x 312 pixels
- Shared* image in post: 1200 x 630 pixels

This is an image you add to your posts.

Season your page with keywords and contact info

Use keywords as, well, a "key" strategy to attract customers to your Facebook page. Keywords are the terms your customers are most likely to type into search engines when looking for your product or service. Sprinkle these keywords throughout the About section of your page, including in both the short description and long description sections.

Include your URL in the About section and on the front page. If a customer does a keyword search and ends up going directly to your Facebook page, you want to make it easy for them to click through to your website.

Activate your Call-to-Action button

When customers get to your Facebook page, what do you want them to do? This is where your Call-to-Action button comes in handy. Every business page comes with a Call-to-Action button in the cover photo area that you can edit to your liking. Do you want people to review your website next or pick up the phone and give you a call? Your Call-to-Action button directs them.

You can use a Call-to-Action to steer your Facebook audience in the direction that meets the goals of your page. Don't miss the opportunity to get potential customers more involved with your business.

Posting on Facebook

Once you've set up your business page, you need to have a game plan for posting updates. If you never post, it won't take long for your customers to forget about your page. This section will give you some important tips for posting effectively.

Call-to-Action Button Choices

Facebook offers the following Call-to-Action button options and allows you to select variations of each:

- Book our Services
- Get in Touch with Us
- Learn More About Us
- Make a Purchase or Donation
- Use Our App or Game

The first rule of posting: mix it up!

Believe it or not, you already have a slew of valuable content to share. For more on this, check out Chapter 7, Editorial Meal Planning, where I talk about mining your existing content sources for social media material. But don't just unimaginatively post what you have. Be creative and repurpose your content into different formats. The same piece of content can be shared many ways: plain text, a text-based graphic, a chart or other data visual, an image and even a video. These days, posts with images or videos, especially, are much more likely to get attention than plain text. Monitor what your audience responds to. Once you know what's getting the most engagement, you can focus on coming up with more posts of that type, but don't get too one-dimensional. People love variety.

Resist the urge to blatantly sell and self-promote

Your Facebook page is not the place to try a hard sell. If you do nothing but pitch your product on Facebook, you will quickly be tuned out. People go on Facebook to communicate with friends and family, be entertained, explore topics they are interested in and maybe even learn something new. In fact, Facebook has announced that if the majority of your posts are promotional pitches, they will significantly limit your reach.

There are thousands of businesses on Facebook that have found ways to reach their audience effectively. Share interesting information about topics that resonate with your audience. Show the character and personality of your business. You will be much more successful when you post meaningful content consistently, and post about product offers or company sales occasionally.

Who Knew?!

Being from a traditional marketing background, and having obtained my MBA in a pre-social media world, I was trained to blare out messages. But working in social media marketing has taught me that louder is not always better. Knowing how to listen and react is what makes businesses successful on Facebook and other social media platforms.

Send traffic to your website

Your Facebook page can be a great tool for sending traffic to your company website. SEO (search engine optimization) techniques help search engines locate and rank your website so your business can be found higher up in the search results. Essentially, every time you link from your Facebook page to your website, you are giving a boost to your SEO. Posts about customer stories, testimonials, blog updates, and company news such as a new product launch are all easy ways to send Facebook users to your website.

Educate your audience

More and more, people log on to Facebook to learn something. Freely sharing information about your product, business or industry establishes you as a knowledgeable source who customers can turn to when they need help or want to learn more. Share updates of your business blog if you have one. If your followers like what you post, they are more likely to share your tips with other potential customers.

Post content consistently

How often should your business post on Facebook? If you asked 10 different social media experts that question, you might get 10 different answers. Some would say once a day, some several times a day and some several times a week. And they all could be right. The truth is, every case is different. Some businesses with a highly engaged audience can post several times a day and every post will get some degree of engagement. Others are better off limiting their activity to a few posts per week. To figure out what's right for your Facebook page, you need to monitor your audience's engagement trends and plan accordingly.

Consistent posting works best, so once you decide on a schedule that works for you, stick with it. Your social media schedule may depend on other marketing action items. For example, if you routinely publish a new blog every Monday, you can plan to share excerpts from it later during the week. The most successful businesses on social media stick to a posting schedule, and their followers know to look for updates at regular times.

Share information and advice you'd give to your favorite customer

Strive to give your Facebook audience something that will improve their life or business in some way. Before posting something, stop and ask yourself if this is what your followers want to get from you. Did your followers "like" your page because they wanted to hear you remind them on a daily basis how wonderful you are? Probably not. Remember to be human. When you chat with your best customers, you don't tell them you are amazing—you show them by being amazing. Make your customers lives' easier by posting helpful advice and insights.

Focus on engagement

Engagement on social media refers to how people respond to your posts. Usually this is by liking, commenting or sharing the post. Being successful on Facebook means generating a lot of engagement with your followers. Are people eating up your content, or leaving your Facebook page hungry? If your followers enjoy your content, you likely have a higher level of engagement. Manage your page in a way that fulfills your audience needs, and you will be rewarded by an increasing number of followers who appreciate your content.

Who Knew?!

Any social media manager will tell you engagement is important. But on Facebook it's especially valuable: every time someone comments on your post, it gets a boost from Facebook's algorithm, and Facebook will show it to more people. The recipe is more comments = longer lifetime of your post = more people see it.

Feeling a bit overwhelmed yet? That's OK. Take a deep breath, drink some coffee (the go-to stress response of us Seattleites) and take the time to set up your Facebook page. In the next section, I've included some techniques for monitoring your account, plus an advanced technique.

Monitor Facebook to Improve Your Recipes

Are your customers sending compliments to the chef, or is their food getting sent back to the kitchen? "Insights" is Facebook's built-in analytics tool to help you understand how your page is doing. By using Facebook Insights, you can learn about your audience's likes and dislikes, problems, worries and values, so you can create content that resonates with them. Here are some tips for understanding your audience on Facebook.

Track your topline metrics monthly

When you first go into the Insights area, you will see some basic metrics, including how many people you have reached, post engagement, and likes within the last week or month. Take note of your page summary metrics. Did your post engagements increase or decrease? How about your views. The Summary is one of my favorite places to get quick feedback on Facebook results.

Taking inventory of these simple metrics helps you determine whether your overall activity is increasing, decreasing or staying consistent.

Evaluate individual posts. What's working?

Insights gives you a quick visual of your recent posts and how well they performed. For a more complete list, go to the Posts link in Insights, as shown below. Look at the reach, clicks and engagement each post received.

Take some time to play detective and see what makes your audience take action. Look at what they share. When people share your post, it shows they value the content and believe it will benefit their followers.

Who is actively engaging with your content?

Facebook Insights allows you to see the demographics of your fans, as well as the demographics of your engaged fans under the People tab. It's more useful to see who is engaging with your content. Those are the folks who are most interested in what you have to say. They want to learn about your business and are more likely to buy from you. Know who they are.

What You Can Learn from Your Facebook Posts

Answer these questions when reviewing your content:

- Which content topics are getting the most reach? What about the best engagement?
- There are four types of post content for Facebook: text, links, photo and video. Which post type is getting the most reach? The most engagement?
- What is the tone of your most popular posts? Are they sharing a feeling? Are they entertaining? Informative?
- When are your posts most popular? What time of day? What days of the week?

Note what's working on a monthly basis and plan for the next month

You're busy, I hear you. But take just 15 minutes to evaluate what is working on your Facebook page at the end of every month. Identify "lessons learned" to carry over to the next month. It's time well spent. Did everyone love your "free kitten giveaway" post, but no one responded to the post about ridding your house of fleas? (This assumes you are running a pet care business, of course). Plan to create more posts that resonate with your audience the following month.

My Favorite Dish: Facebook Live

In early 2016 Facebook jumped on the streaming video trend. Much like Periscope, Facebook Live gives you the ability to live stream video right from your mobile device to a Facebook audience. This opens up possibilities galore for connecting with your audience and showing the fun, approachable and human side of your brand. And the beauty of it is that businesses of any size can take advantage of Facebook Live. There is no extra fee, no new apps to learn, and nothing to download. Simply use your existing Facebook page to get started.

Live video won't be for everyone – many small business owners will feel a bit camera shy and not ready to present their business in such a casual and spontaneous style. But for those who embrace it, Facebook offers a change to talk to your customers your authentic self. Your Facebook fans will enjoy the opportunity to get to know the people behind the brand. If you can get past the stage fright of being on camera there are so many ways to stand apart of your competition.

Although the "how" of Facebook Live shouldn't give you much trouble, the "what" of your broadcasting plan might be a bit trickier. Here are some ideas for how small businesses can make the most of Facebook Live.

Offer a behind-the-scenes tour

Are your customers curious about how you make your products and the ins and outs of your business? Give them a behind the scenes tour that shows how it all comes together. This is especially effective if you are planning an event or setting up for a party. People will feel like they are part of the action before they get to the actual event.

Give them a live demo

Do you have tips for using your service or product that you want to share? Give a live demo of how to use your product from start to finish and answer any questions that come up right then and there. Take this idea a step further and plan an "unboxing" of your new product during a product launch and help your audience learn how to set it up and get started.

Do a quick DIY course

There is a reason that YouTube is considered the second largest search engine after Google. People like to learn through videos. Think of easy videos you can record that will resonate with your audience and plan a series of mini-classes. A restaurant could stream a video of its chef making a simple dish. A hardware store could show how to repair a dishwasher.

Share a customer story

Invite a customer who has used your product or service to solve a business challenge to join you in a Facebook Live session. This is a great opportunity to address common challenges faced by your customers. Give your audience a chance to ask questions that you or your customer can answer. This lets you have both a Q&A session with your audience and a great customer testimonial.

Bring your business to your customer

Do you have a physical storefront? Walk down the aisles using Facebook Live and show your customers what's going on sale. You can even offer a special Facebook Live Deal with a special discount if they come in within a certain time frame and mention your video.

The list of potential uses for Facebook Live goes on and on. You're only limited by your creativity! And keep in mind that after you broadcast, your video will go on your timeline so people can see and comment on it for days and weeks to come.

Chapter 2
LinkedIn:
Let's Do Lunch

106 million
monthly
active users

25% of US adults
are on LinkedIn

Check Please!

45% of US adults
earning over $75,000
per year use LinkedIn

LINKEDIN MENU

Business Lunch for Busy Professionals!

Intro to LinkedIn

PAGE + PROFILE

POSTING

MONITOR LINKEDIN
TO IMPROVE YOUR RECIPES

MY FAVORITE DISH:
GROW EXPOSURE WITH
LINKEDIN PUBLISHING

Intro to LinkedIn

The flavor of LinkedIn

If you could take a networking "meet and greet" event and transfer it to an online setting, you would end up with something that looks a lot like LinkedIn: professional, purposeful and an opportunity to show off your best self. Most people know LinkedIn as a platform for personal networking with other professionals, but it's also a powerful tool for getting more company exposure and brand recognition. The tone of LinkedIn is more business-like than other social media platforms.

Should LinkedIn be on your menu?

All professionals should have an individual profile on LinkedIn. Your business should also have a company page. LinkedIn company pages don't require the same level of maintenance as Facebook business pages. Check in periodically to ensure your business profile is stable, but focus your valuable time and energy on the platforms that best reach your target audience.

Facts and figures

There are more 106 monthly active users on LinkedIn. The professionalism of LinkedIn attracts an older audience than the other platforms. As the bar chart shows, LinkedIn is visited by 33% of people age 30 to 49. In addition, LinkedIn users then to have a high level of education and a higher income level.[3]

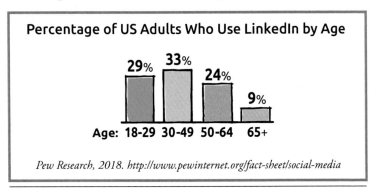

Percentage of US Adults Who Use LinkedIn by Age

29% 33% 24% 9%

Age: 18-29 30-49 50-64 65+

Pew Research, 2018. http://www.pewinternet.org/fact-sheet/social-media

Your LinkedIn Page and Profile

Wondering how to dive into the world of LinkedIn? This section offers tips for you and your business to get the best out of this social media platform.

Optimize your personal profile for search

Just like its good practice to optimize your website so it can be easily found, it's important to optimize your personal LinkedIn profile. Think of LinkedIn as a search engine. What search terms would people use on Google to find you and your business? Those are your keywords, and they belong in your LinkedIn introduction summary and headlines, as well as in the skills and expertise sections of your profile. Google will pull only the first 156 characters of your LinkedIn description in search results. Place your best keywords in the beginning.

Use a professional personal photo

Put your best foot forward on LinkedIn. Don't use a blurry photo of you at a party, with the person next to you clearly cropped out. On LinkedIn, you need to take it up a notch. Use a professionally taken personal photo, or a professional headshot if you have one. According to LinkedIn's statistics, using a professional photo will get you seven times more views than a casual one.

The optimal size for personal photos is between 200 × 200 and 500 × 500 pixels. Use a recent photo so people will recognize you when they see you in person. Your LinkedIn profile should also be current. Link your profile to your company website, blog and other social media accounts. Double check your contact information is up to date every few months. You will also need a background photo. Be creative here and choose something that reflects you and your business.

Claim your customized URL

When you first set up your LinkedIn profile, you will get a default profile link that looks like a gobbledygook of random characters. The good news is you can claim a customized URL that includes your name. To do this, scroll over the URL located under the photo on your profile page. A little cogwheel icon will appear next to the URL. Click on it to select a customized URL. Many people add this customized URL to a business card in order to grow their connections.

Key Ingredients for LinkedIn Personal Profiles Images

- Personal page profile image: Between 400 x 400 to 20,000 x 20,000 pixels
- Personal background image: 1,584 x 396 pixels

Build a powerful company page

A LinkedIn company page can give your business more exposure and allows followers to learn more about your company. Company pages look very plain if you do just the bare minimum, so it's important to add many of the bells and whistles LinkedIn offers. There is an area to describe your business, but you will need to do a lot with a little space there. All LinkedIn gives you is about three lines of text, a list of specialties, and some other basic company info. After that, it is up to you to embellish your page with frequent updates, media and showcase pages.

At this time, you can only comment and post in the LinkedIn newsfeed as your individual profile, not as your company profile. You can, however, share posts from your LinkedIn company page. Take advantage of this capability in order to bring more exposure to your company.

Create one (or more!) showcase pages

Showcase pages are sub-pages of your company page with more details about your business. Highlight your most prominent services and projects, release free guides and special offers, or share other promotional features on your showcase pages. People can follow these pages just like they follow your company page. Any showcase pages you create will appear on the right column of your company pages, so visitors can scroll down to learn more about your company.

Setting up a showcase page is similar to setting up a company page. You will be prompted to pick a category, enter a name and description, and upload a couple of images. The square image you upload will appear next to your showcase page links, so customize it to describe what your page is about. The huge "hero"

Key Ingredientsfor LinkedIn Company Page Images

- Company page cover image: min 1,536 x 768 pixels
- Logo size: 300 x 300 pixels
- Square logo: 60 x 60 pixels
- Cover image for showcase page: 1,536 x 768 pixels

image acts as a backdrop of your showcase page. Use an image that reflects your brand, and add a text overlay to describe the contents of your showcase page.

Posting on LinkedIn

Ask people to endorse you and give you recommendations

This is a "must do" for LinkedIn. Not only does this demonstrate your expertise in your niche, but when people give you a recommendation, you can use it (with permission) on your website and sales collateral. Just like millions of people look up Yelp recommendations before they try a new restaurant, many people check out a person's LinkedIn reviews before they decide to work with them.

Post updates regularly that resonate with your audience

The key here is to share meaningful and helpful updates with your connections, and do so regularly. Align your updates with your followers' needs and interests so they see you as someone who has a lot of experience in your field. Share content regularly so you are more likely to show up in your followers' stream of updates. I always advise my clients to use an editorial calendar to manage their LinkedIn updates as much as possible. When you have a preplanned list of topics to talk about, it's easier to share consistently. I include more tips on planning your social media content in Chapter 7.

Share posts with images, videos and links

It's more likely your posts will get noticed if they are accompanied by an enticing photo or video. In fact, LinkedIn videos have a 75% higher reach percentage. Sharing your presentations from SlideShare is another great way to communicate with your audience. You're able to add rich media—both in your posts and embedded on your profile page. SlideShare (www.slideshare.net) is a presentation network owned by LinkedIn where professionals can share their slide presentations in private or public profiles.

Be ACTIVE!

Comment on others' feeds to encourage interaction. When you comment, like or share news posted by others, they are likely to do the same for you. LinkedIn makes this extra easy by prompting you with some quick updates in the upper-right corner of your home page when you log in. It only takes a few seconds to like or comment on one of your connection's updates.

Make new connections often

If you have someone's business email, you can connect with them on LinkedIn. You can also add people as connections after

Head Chef:
Four Seasons Hotels and Resorts

Four Seasons Hotels and Resorts Four Seasons Mini Olympics 2016 - Four Seasons Resort Mauritius at Anahita recently organized a Mini Olympics for their team. Employees competed in in 11 different games from a sac race to beach soccer – a day full of excitement. Finally, the green team got to lift the big trophy – but everyone felt like winners having enjoyed a great day out! Go Team Mauritius!

FS Mini Olympics 2016

Green Team - Winner

Team Spirit is the motto!

Best Captain

Like (375) · Comment (3) · Share · 1 month ago

The Four Seasons Hotels and Resorts shared highlights from the year by running a series of updates with photos and descriptions of their favorite moments. It was a great way to keep their brand top of mind on LinkedIn during the holiday (travel) season and also to humanize their brand.

collecting their business cards at a conference or networking event. In addition, the LinkedIn user interface does a great job of suggesting people to add to your network. Make it part of your schedule to check your LinkedIn account and look for new connections. When you send a connection request via LinkedIn, edit the default message with a reminder of how you met. People are quicker to respond to a personal message than they are to a canned connection request.

Be exact with image sizing

Last but not least: LinkedIn is pretty fussy about image sizes, so size your images correctly before you try to publish them on your personal or company page. See the size requirements in the box below.

Explore LinkedIn Native or Live Stream Video

LinkedIn rolled out native and live stream video in 2017. Sharing a video in the LinkedIn newsfeed allows your LinkedIn connections to get a better sense of who you are if you haven't met face to face. You can pre-record a video, edit and upload it or you can use your phone to record yourself. Videos uploaded natively must be at least three seconds and no more than 10 minutes, with the ideal video length being about three minutes. Live stream videos are currently limited to under one minute. Enhance your video with a short description to tell people why they should watch your video. In the description you can tag others, add links and hashtags.

Monitor LinkedIn to Improve Your Recipes

———

LinkedIn has come a long way in beefing up their analytics tools, so you can see how your personal profile and your company page are performing. As with most social media platforms, the more active you are, the more you are going to see a return in engagement and attention to your account. Monitoring your metrics will help you understand who is seeing your messages and how they are responding.

LinkedIn has metrics for both your personal and company accounts. We will cover both in this section.

Pay attention to your topline metrics on your personal profile dashboard

LinkedIn makes it easy to see your recent activity at a glance, with a simple dashboard of your personal profile analytics on the top of your page when you log on.

This quick peek lists your number of connections and provides a link to tools to expand your network. It also tells you how many people have visited your profile in the last 90 days and allows you to click through for more details. Click through to find out how many people have viewed your profile.

Go to your profile view by clicking on your photo, then scroll down to your dashboard. This dashboard can only be seen by you when you're logged in. It gives you topline metrics of who has viewed your profile, your article views, and who has found you through a LinkedIn search in the last 90 days. Explore any of these topics by clicking through to get details.

Keep an eye on topline metrics for your company page

LinkedIn's pace is decidedly slower than other social media platforms. Despite that, it's useful to check in each month to see who has followed your company page. Take note of the following:

- How many followers do you have?
- How many followers did you gain or lose during the month?
- What is the demographic of the people following you?

You can find these simple metrics by going to your company page and then clicking on the Analytics tab. Edit the date range to view recent data versus a large-scale snapshot of your follower growth.

Monitor the response of your updates

When reviewing your company page metrics, it is useful to evaluate the response to your updates. Go to your company page analytics area to see a list of posts you have shared as your company and what kinds of responses they received.

LinkedIn tracks your visitors, updates, and followers. Plus, you can see if they found you on a desktop or mobile device.

When you go to the Analytics tab, you will also see a list of your posts. The default view is the last 15 days, but you can reset the range to as much as 6 months to get a broader view. This page shares reach, engagement and follower details.

What You Can Learn from LinkedIn Publishing Metrics:

Answer these questions when reviewing your content:

- What blog topics are getting the most views?
- What blog topics are getting the most engagement?
- What are the job titles and industries of the people engaging in your posts?
- Who are your top engagers?

Understand who your audience is

There are a couple of ways to evaluate who your audience is and if they are your target audience. You can view both the demographics of your blog readers and the demographics of your company page followers.

As you build your LinkedIn following and become more active, you will also grow your followers. You aren't likely to have as many followers on LinkedIn as you do on other social media platforms, but it is useful to see the demographics of those who are following you. Look at your following to see how they compare in terms of seniority, industry, company size and business function. You can view this data by choosing any time span between one day to a 12-month date range.

Discover who is visiting your company page

Similar to seeing who is following you, you can also look at who is visiting your page and when. This is especially interesting when you want to learn which marketing activities are driving people to your LinkedIn site. Many businesses find when they increase activity on their LinkedIn account, publish an article or run LinkedIn ads, they see a bump in their company page visits.

Make note of what's working and plan ahead

The average LinkedIn user is only active on LinkedIn once a week, but the more you use LinkedIn to promote your company, the more you will want to check your stats. Watch your metrics to decide if your following is growing due to your publishing activity, updates, or the personal connections you are making. Did you notice a spike in profile views or new company page followers when you posted a new article? If so, make time in your schedule next month to do it more often.

As I have said before, there is no one recipe for social media marketing. LinkedIn gives you an opportunity to network socially on behalf of your company and yourself. Test what activities work for you in both areas and then integrate them into your strategy.

My Favorite Dish: Grow Exposure with LinkedIn Publishing

LinkedIn has its own content publishing platform. Articles show up in the LinkedIn news stream and are seen by those who follow you, similar to updates. But the reach goes further than that. LinkedIn will notify each of your connections when you publish on its platform. The articles are also shared in a directory and are searchable via Google. Since articles are hosted on an established platform with high optimization, their potential reach is much broader.

Getting started is easy. As of this printing, you can find it by clicking the "Write an article" button on your homepage. Right now, you publish from your personal profile, not your company page, although that may change in the future. The interface is simple to use and gives you the opportunity to add a cover image, as well as tags so your article can be accurately categorized and found by the people who would be most interested in it.

What should you share? Articles about your industry or niche, insights and commentary on recent news or statistics, problems your business can solve… really, anything you would put on your own blog or present at an industry conference.

Don't be salesy

LinkedIn's publishing platform is not the place to make a sales pitch. If you just go out with a commercial, you will lose credibility. People read your posts because they are interested in the topic or your expertise. They aren't expecting to be sold to, and this is simply not the place to try.

Think about your reader

Remember the people who will read your articles are generally educated, professional and looking for information to help them in their work. Your articles should deliver value to satisfy them. With every post, you should aim to help your reader solve a problem.

Provide "meaty" content

In the '80s, a fast food hamburger chain ran "Where's the beef?" TV commercials, in which customers were dissatisfied with their tiny sized hamburger patty and wanted more meat. It's the same with publishing on LinkedIn. People are looking for solid, helpful, expert content. Add multimedia such as images, links, SlideShare presentations or videos to illustrate your points. Just don't serve up fluffy, vague blog content.

Include a Call-to-Action

While it's not ok to deliver a sales pitch, it's acceptable to include a Call-to-Action and direct your reader where to go to learn more. For example, you can send them to your website or a landing page where they can download or purchase your eBook. LinkedIn publishing is the perfect place to tell them how to take the next step to learn more about your industry or business.

Chapter 3
Twitter:
Dinner on the Go

336 million
monthly
active users

24% of US adults are
on Twitter

Check Please!

32% of US adults
earning over $75,000
per year use Twitter

Sources: http://www.pewinternet.org/2018/03/01/social-media-use-in-2018/ ; https://www.statista.com/statistics/274564/monthly-active-twitter-users-in-the-united-states/. Accessed October 8, 2018.

TWITTER MENU

The Fastest of Fast Food!

Intro to Twitter

PAGE + PROFILE

POSTING

POSTING

Continued

MONITOR TWITTER
TO IMPROVE YOUR RECIPES

MY FAVORITE DISH:
HOSTING A TWITTER CHAT

Intro to Twitter

The flavor of Twitter

Twitter is a microblogging platform that allows users to broadcast very short snippets of content in 280 characters or less. (That's characters, not words!) Twitter is very busy, and you need to be active to be successful on Twitter. This means you need to post, repost and interact with others. Users post a combination of images, links, video, text and hashtags to get the most out of their 280-character limit.

Businesses and professionals use Twitter in a variety of ways. Some use it as an outlet for frequent news and updates about their businesses, giving people a behind-the-scenes look at what is going on. Some are more formal, announcing press releases and other more polished information about their company. And some use Twitter primarily as a learning tool: they watch for industry news using hashtags and keywords, and retweet what they like.

Should Twitter be on your menu?

Twitter is a wonderful place for up-to-the-minute news. If you can keep up with the trends and news surrounding your industry, Twitter folks will appreciate it. Some of the top industries sharing news on Twitter include tech, sports, business, health and politics, but the list truly goes on and on.

Find others in your business niche with Twitter. By searching and using industry hashtags, you can connect with influencers, prospective customers and potential partners all over the world. Whether you are learning from others, conversing with others or sharing what you know, Twitter allows small businesses to have a big reach.

Facts and figures

Twitter was once one of the largest social media platforms in number of users, but it was surpassed by Instagram in late 2015. As of March 2018, Statista reported Twitter had more than 336 million monthly active users worldwide. As shown below, a relatively young adult audience flocks to Twitter, with 45% of US adults age 18 to 29 being active.

There are slightly more men using Twitter than women (24% of men and 21% of women). Only 30% of Twitter users have graduated college, which may be due to Twitter having a younger audience. In terms of income, 27% of adults who make over $75,000 and 27% of adults who make $50,000-$74,999 are on Twitter. A full 79% of Twitter accounts lie outside the US, with the site supporting 40 languages.[4]

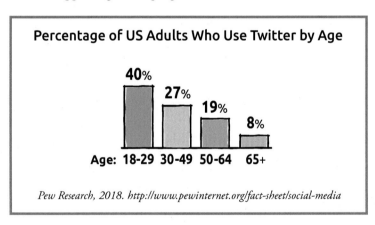

Percentage of US Adults Who Use Twitter by Age

40% 27% 19% 8%

Age: 18-29 30-49 50-64 65+

Pew Research, 2018. http://www.pewinternet.org/fact-sheet/social-media

Your Twitter Page and Profile: The Basic Ingredients

Tell people why they should follow you in your profile

A Twitter bio only allows for 160 characters of text, so make every character count. Tell your audience what's in it for them if they follow you. Will you share insightful quotes? Give helpful advice about your products? Cover the latest industry news? Or maybe all of the above? Decide why it's worth following you and say it in your profile description. (But keep it short!)

Make your photo approachable

Twitter is a casual space. People want to interact with others on Twitter more than they want to talk to brands and logos. That being said, they understand businesses have a social media presence, too, and there are real people behind every brand.

It's fine if your profile photo is a logo, but show the clever, interesting, smart, helpful and personable human being behind the brand. People would rather follow a person they know something about than follow an impersonal brand. If you are the main face of your small business and want to incorporate your logo, consider a photo of you holding a sign with your logo on it.

Posting on Twitter

Expect to cook up a lot of content

It's important to be active on Twitter. One of the quickest ways to lose followers is inactivity. There are at least half a dozen Twitter apps created to manage your Twitter account that tell you who to unfollow. Posting three times a day and engaging twice a day is optimal for my business. This lets me slowly build my following and interact with current followers. Your industry may move faster or slower. Start with a schedule you can manage and then watch to see if you need to adjust your activity level.

Key Ingredients for Twitter

- Profile image: 400 x 400 pixels (displays as 200 x 200)
- Header image: 1,500 x 500 pixels
- In-stream image: 440 x 220 pixels

Add images and video to your tweets

Tweets with photos get an average of five times more engagement than text tweets alone. To get the best results, you need to post images natively—in other words, upload the image directly to Twitter rather than sharing through another app, like Instagram. Otherwise you risk having your images show up as just links. You can post images of any size on Twitter, but in the mobile view they will be cropped to 440 x 220, since most people view Twitter on a mobile device.

Provide man-on-the-street updates at events

People go to Twitter for fast news. It has redefined the way media works, with mainstream media now providing coverage on Twitter in addition to their traditional outlets. Twitter is especially useful and popular for events. Take advantage of this trend and ask yourself: what events in your industry can you "cover" with live updates for your followers? You might tweet out photos, breaking news or product announcements. Look for opportunities to be the "man on the street."

Organize your followers with lists

Like a cook who creates multiple dishes at once, you need organization in your kitchen. Once you get rolling in the Twittersphere, you will find it virtually impossible to listen to individuals if you don't use Twitter Lists. Twitter lists can be public or private. When you put someone on a public list, they receive a notification from Twitter. How you name your lists is important. If you add someone to a list called "Morons I met" (which I know you would never do), they will know, and probably won't be too pleased. If you add people to a list called "Cool people from Meetup," they will see it and pat themselves on the back for being considered so cool. Make a list strategy before you start adding people. Here are some suggested list names to get you started.

And, of course, this is Twitter, so you have to comply with character limits. List names are limited to 25 characters.

Connect on Twitter as an event follow-up

The best way to build a quality following on Twitter is to do what I call "Growing in Meaningful Spurts." Events provide an easy way do just that. For instance, are you planning on going to a conference where you will exchange business cards? Many people list their Twitter handle on their business cards. After the event, follow them on Twitter, add them to a list and send a quick note saying it was nice to meet them.

Who Knew?!

When I first joined Twitter I was decidedly more passive and used it mostly to keep a pulse on social media marketing news. Over time, I graduated to interacting with others, curating content and letting my personality show a bit more. It's now my go-to resource for connecting with other social media marketing thought leaders. For example, when I listen to a webinar I like, I almost always jump onto Twitter to give feedback to the speaker. I am always surprised at how quickly they respond. People love it when you offer support and feedback on their blogs, webinars, etc., and Twitter is an easy way to do it.

Collaborate with other cooks: participate in Twitter Chats

Nothing shows the power of Twitter's conversation capabilities and expansive reach (yet ability to focus on a specific niche) like Twitter Chats. Also referred to as "Twitter Parties," which, admittedly, does sound more fun, these are online Twitter events in which the participants use a specific hashtag to discuss a topic. Twitter Chats are organized at a specific time and date. Some are reoccurring, while others are one-time events. If you want to find some Twitter Chats, a quick Google search can give you a list that matches your interest and industry. You are likely to enjoy yourself and learn something new, whether you are an active participant or just quietly watching the conversation unfold. If you dare to be an active participant, you will meet people you can connect with after the chat.

Sample Twitter List Names

- Met at Meetup
- Industry influencer
- Local Seattle biz
- Bloggers I follow
- Great tech podcasts
- Our awesome clients

Learn to love hashtags

The ubiquitous # symbol, once known as the "pound sign," has become one of the biggest social media tools in use today. Hashtags are words you tack on to the end of your social media post, such as #catlover or #digitalmarketing. When your hashtagged message goes out into the great universe of social media-ness, people who search the hashtag can find your content. They have an opportunity to follow you, respond or just listen in on the conversation.

Use hashtags to extend the reach of your message

By adding a hashtag to your post, you may capture the attention of those who might not otherwise see your message. Hashtags can be embedded into your messaging for promotions, events, Twitter chats, infographics, images and any other place you can imagine. And they aren't just limited to digital media. Hashtags are also used to promote products and brands anywhere—from billboards to sports signage to TV commercials. Don't overdo it though. On Twitter, it's common to use two or three hashtags per post, whereas on Instagram, the average is thirteen.

Head Chef: Edinburgh Police

The Edinburgh Police wanted to remind their community to protect themselves against break-ins, so they created a series of Lego scenarios in their Twitter posts to make their point.

 EdinburghWestPolice ✔
@EdinPolSW

 Follow

(1/2)Lock yer tools away n keep them oot o' view Having em on display makes it easy fur the housebreaking crew#OpRac

3:01 AM - 10 Apr 2015

↩ 27 ♥ 12

Head Chef: Domino's Pizza

Domino's Pizza UK ✓
@Dominos_UK

🐦 Follow

Domino's Tweet Treat has begun! Include #letsdolunch in your tweets to knock money of our Pep Passion. Full details on.fb.me/Aj8e5P

5 Mar 12

↩ Reply ⟲ Retweet ★ Favorite

Domino's Pizza UK used a #LetsDoLunch promotion that gave Twitter followers a discount when they shared its hashtag.

Search by hashtags to measure the pulse in your industry

Become familiar with the hashtags commonly used for your industry and follow them. For example, when I want the latest technology news on Twitter, I search with the #technews hashtag. It's a simple way to monitor what is going on at any given moment, whether it be news, tips, products, images, videos, webinars, etc. By using an aggregator like Tagboard or Hashtracking, you can get a quick read on the latest postings.

Create your own branded hashtag

Want to create your own following with hashtags rather than sharing the glory with others? No problem. You can go big time and create and use your own branded hashtag. You see this with sports and movies quite a bit. Do some research to confirm others aren't already using your hashtag. Also, be ready to put a lot of marketing and branding effort into promoting and managing the hashtag to keep it alive.

Explore Live Video

Since Twitter purchased Periscope, you can use the Live Video function in Twitter. The video will be accessible on both Twitter and Periscope. Your live videos will automatically be posted as a tweet.

Monitor Twitter to Improve Your Recipes

Content on Twitter moves fast! Check your account regularly to see if your content is hitting the mark and whether you are growing your following in a way that reaches your goals.

Track your topline Tweets and mentions monthly

Most of us know how often we are tweeting, but at the top of your Twitter Analytics account, you can track your tweet activity in a 28-day summary to see how your activity compares to previous months. You can also get a quick read on your tweet impressions, profile visits, mentions and followers with this top dashboard metric.

Monitoring your mentions (every time your handle is used with the @ symbol) is a simple barometer to track your engagement level, since all public conversations on Twitter include mentions. The fastest way to build up mentions is to have conversations on Twitter, retweet others, ask questions, and, well… be social.

Evaluate your Tweet Highlights to see what's working

Your Top Tweets are considered "top" because of the impressions, i.e., how many views you get. The more people who retweet or engage with your content, the more impressions you will receive.

Take a long hard look at each month's Top Tweets. This shows what you are doing right and what you need to do more of. As your account grows, you will see those numbers increase with more engagements.

Drill down to evaluate individual tweets

Click on the Tweets tab in analytics to see how many impressions and how much engagement your individual Tweets have received.

This is where you can scan the hashtags you're using to see if they are getting you the reach and engagement you want.

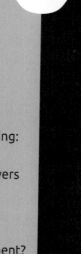

What Can You Learn from Your Tweets?

Answer these questions when reviewing your content:

- What is the topic of the Tweets getting the best reach?
- What is the topic of Tweets getting the best engagement?
- What type of engagements are your Tweets getting: comments or likes?
- What type of Tweets are encouraging your followers to comment?
- What visual components are getting the most engagement: photos or videos?
- When are your Tweets getting the most engagement? What time of day? What day of the week?
- Which hashtags or hashtag combinations seem to get you the most response?

Recognize who your Top Followers are and review follower demographics

Your monthly Top Follower is the Twitter user with the largest following who began following you within the month. Why do you care? Because they have influence and recently decided to follow you. If your Top Followers retweet your content, it will spread exponentially, so it is ideal to cultivate a relationship with these users.

After reviewing your topline numbers, it's worth your time to click over to the Audiences tab on the Analytics menu and look at the demographics of your followers.

Take a moment to evaluate whether your followers fit your target audience. Do they have interests and backgrounds similar to your target market? If you are doing a good job of consistently sharing and curating valuable content in your niche or industry, it's likely your followers share your interests. If you notice several months of followers who really don't match your interests, you need to go back and take a look at what you are sharing to see if it's on target.

For example, my Twitter followers are mostly interested in marketing, technology and entrepreneurship—the ideal people I want to connect with on Twitter.

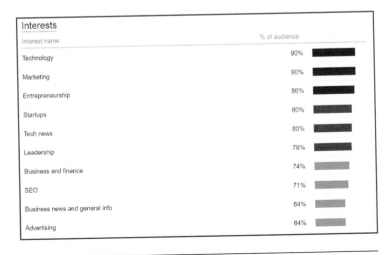

Note what's working on a monthly basis and plan for the next month

As I said before, Twitter moves fast, so you need to stay on your toes to keep up. What's popular one month may not be the next. If you continue to evaluate your account and how it is growing, you will see overall trends and find out what's working for you.

My Favorite Dish: Hosting a Twitter Chat

Since Twitter is the ultimate platform for engaging in social media conversations, it only makes sense there would be organized Twitter Chats to let people with similar interests connect. Twitter Chats provide an opportunity for small businesses to get a conversation going around related topics.

Why Host a Twitter Chat?

Hosting and managing a Twitter Chat is worth your time for several reasons. Participants on the chat are a captive audience who will likely stay tuned in as long as the chat lasts, and possibly afterwards as well, if you offer follow-up content.

Leading Twitter Chats also allows others to become aware of your business. Interact with prospective customers, potential business partners and influencers you might not otherwise reach. Lead the conversation and share valuable content with your audience to position yourself as a community leader. Your audience will begin to tune in to your chats if you host them regularly. On a fast-moving, hashtag-centric platform like Twitter, you have the opportunity to go viral quickly.

Tips for managing effective Twitter Chats

Promote the event in advance. Create multiple tweets announcing the chat to your followers, scheduled at a variety of days and times.

Announce through multiple channels. Share news of your chat on all your social media platforms and inform people on your email list. You can even mention it on your website. Create eye-catching graphics to draw more attention to your announcements.

Ask guests to share. If your chat will include guest speakers, ask them to promote it. Give them promotional language or images they can use. Likewise, reach out to key influencers to help spread the word.

Content is king. Focus on compelling content containing facts and stories you know your audience will value.

Provide a framework without being too scripted. Twitter chats have a casual nature, so you don't want the conversation to feel canned, though you should be well prepared. Before starting the chat, create a framework you can refer to as it unfolds. This will help you remember important points.

Have plenty of questions. Prepare a list of questions ahead of time around your topic. About ten questions are ideal for a one-hour chat, but have some extras on hand in case you need them. It is better to have extra content than to run out early.

Use tools to manage the conversation. Tools like Tweet Chat or Hootsuite can help you focus more productively on the conversation stream and watch out for questions that need to be answered.

Think quality over quantity. It's better to have fewer people actively contributing than lots of people just passing through and not listening.

Recognize loyal followers. There are probably people who regularly engage in your community. Welcome them in, retweet their quality content and answer their questions.

Capture a transcript. Use a tool like Storify to capture the transcript easily. During the chat, "like" the Tweets you want to include in your transcript so it's easier to find them later.

Summarize the chat with a blog. It's hard for participants to see all the contributions on a Twitter Chat as it's happening. Summarize the chat and post the collective insights in a follow-up blog. Share the link with people who were active in the chat.

Measure and evaluate afterwards. A tool like Hashtracking.com will help you measure metrics, such as hashtag reach, activity, top tweeters and other hashtags that were used. What questions did people answer the most? Did other topics come up to cover in another Twitter chat or blog? You can use this data to learn more about your audience's interests and to plan future chats.

Madalyn Sklar is a Twitter expert and hosts Twitter chats every week. I had the pleasure of being a guest on her #TwitterSmarter chat and we followed up with a Facebook Live video interview to discuss the highlights.